Karnataka

Ranee Vijaya Kuttaiah

NEW DAWN PRESS, INC.
USA• UK• INDIA

NEW DAWN PRESS GROUP

Published by New Dawn Press Group
New Dawn Press, Inc., 244 South Randall Rd # 90, Elgin, IL 60123
e-mail: sales@newdawnpress.com

New Dawn Press, 2 Tintern Close, Slough, Berkshire, SL1-2TB, UK
e-mail: ndpuk@newdawnpress.com

New Dawn Press (An Imprint of Sterling Publishers (P) Ltd.)
A-59, Okhla Industrial Area, Phase-II, New Delhi-110020
e-mail: info@sterlingpublishers.com; www.sterlingpublishers.com

Karnataka Cuisine
© 2005, Ranee Vijaya Kuttaiah
ISBN 1 84557 239 4

Published by Sterling Publishers Pvt. Ltd., New Delhi-110020.
Lasertypeset by Vikas Compographics, New Delhi-110020.
Printed at Sai Early Learners (P) Ltd., New Delhi-110020.

About the book

Endowed with amazing natural beauty and a delightful variety of cuisine, Karnataka has often been referred to as a culinary paradise by discerning lovers of good food. This book presents some of the most mouthwatering delicacies whose recipes have been culled from different parts of the state.

Each region has its own distinct and unique cuisine, and I have compiled a wide-ranging collection, including the purely vegetarian Lingayat cuisine, the Gowda cuisine and the Bunt and Madhwa Brahmin cuisine of Mangalore.

I proudly present my third book which is of my state. A beautiful song says "Chelova Kannadanadu, Udaya Vagali Nama" – in other words, Karnataka defies beauty and grace. It is a home you have returned to. May the state of Karnataka, land of plenty, always radiate charm, contentment, peace and hospitality.

I dedicate this book to the Kannadigas, whose culture is ever famous.

Ranee Vijaya Kuttaiah

For my son
DEVAYA

Contents

Glossary

Akki	- Rice or rice flour	Bhat	- Rice
Aloogadai	- Potato	Bisebelli	- Hot dhall
Anna	- Rice	Copra	- Dry coconut
Avalakki	- Beaten rice	Gojju	- A thick chutney-like curry
Avarai Belai	- Broad country beans	Handi	- Pork
		Hasiru	- Green
Avarai Kalu	- Dried broad beans	Hulli	- Curry
Badanaikai	- Aubergine	Hunsae	- Tamarind
Badu	- Dry fried	Hurida	- Fried
Basalae	- Thick green edible creeper grown in certain areas	Huruli	- Horse gram
		Kadalai	- Chickpeas
		Kanji	- Watery rice
Batani	- Peas	Kas kas	- Poppy seeds
Bayraikai Sopu	- A mixture of various types of Indian greens except spinach and sag.	Koli	- Chicken
		Kuttu	- Mixed curry
		Lobia	- Black-eyed peas
		Madikai Kalu	- Dry kidney beans
		Majigai	- Curds

6

Mamsa	- Mutton	Samba	- Small-grained, sweet-smelling rice
Meenu	- Fish		
Mensau	- Chillies	Sambar powder	- A mixture of ground spices available in Indian stores
Mentai	- Fenugreek		
Neer	- Water		
Neeru Soopu Saru	- Watery green curry	Saru	- Gravy
		Thelli Saru	- Curry made with pulses
Nimbai	- Lemon	Thoor Dhall	- Red gram
Paliya	- Dry vegetables	Upensa Saru	- Salty dhall curry
Sagu	- Vegetable	Vana Menchinkai	- Red chilli
		Vanna Meenu	- Dry fish

VEGETABLES

Aubergine	- Baingan	Lady's finger	- Bhindi
Capsicum	- Shimla mirch	Onion	- Piaz
Carrot	- Gajar	Peas	- Matar
Cauliflower	- Phool gobhi	Tomato	- Tamatar
Green chilli	- Hari mirch		

HERBS & SPICES

Asafoetida	- Hing	Cardamom	- Elaichi
Black pepper	- Kali mirch	Cinnamon	- Dalchini

Clove	- Laung	Mint leaves	- Pudina ke pattey
Cumin seed	- Zeera	Mustard	- Rai
Fenugreek	- Methi	Tamarind	- Imli
Garlic	- Lahsun	Turmeric powder	- Haldi

MISCELLANEOUS

Almond	- Badam	Maize flour	- Makki ka atta
Bengal gram lentil	- Chana dhall	Raisins	- Kishmish
		Rice flour	- Chawal ka atta
Cashewnut	- Kaju	Saffron	- Jafraan
Chickpea	- Kabuli chana	Semolina	- Suji or rava
Clarified butter	- Ghee	Split black gram lentil	- Urad dhall
Gram flour	- Besan		
Jackfruit	- Kathal	Split green gram lentil	- Moong dhall
Jaggery	- Gur		

Garam Masala: Mixture of coriander, cloves, cinnamon, cardamom, cumin, peppercorn and nutmeg.

Taal Masala Powder: ½ kg Mangalore red chilli, ½ kg red chilli, 5 tbsp coriander seeds, 2 tbsp cumin seeds, 2 tbsp fenugreek seeds, 2 tbsp black pepper. Roast all the above ingredients lightly and powder them. Store in a bottle.

Akki Roti

Akki Roti

Ingredients

3 glasses rice flour
¼ tsp salt
¾ glass water

Method

1. Knead the flour with all the ingredients into a smooth dough.
2. Make small lemon-sized balls, and with the palm of your hand, flatten them into thin round discs on a dry plastic sheet or a wet muslin cloth. Pat constantly till the disc becomes thin like a roti.
3. Heat a griddle and place the roti on it. Roast one side and turn it over. Keep patting both sides with a clean, wet cloth while roasting. While tossing the roti, smear the tawa with dry rice flour.
4. **Variation:** Maize flour or ragi flour can also be used.

Paddu

Ingredients

2 cups rice, soaked
1 cup black gram, soaked
¼ tsp baking soda
Paddin Kalu to make the paddus
Salt to taste

Method

1. Soak the rice and gram for 8 hours. Add the baking soda.

2. Then grind to make into a thick dosa batter, adding salt to taste. Keep overnight to ferment.

3. Lightly grease the moulds of the Paddin Kalu* with cooking oil and keep it for a day.

4. Place the Paddin Kalu over heat. When hot, pour the mixture into the moulds with the help of a shallow spoon and close the lid. Cook till it turns light golden brown in colour.

5. Remove it slowly from the moulds. Serve hot.

---

* Paddin Kalu is a vessel made of stoneware with deep moulds. The number of the moulds are four or six. It is available in all cookware stores in South India.

Copra Chutney

Ingredients

½ coconut, scraped
4 green chillies
1 small bunch coriander leaves
1 sprig curry leaves
5 cloves garlic
Salt and sugar to taste

For the seasoning

1 tsp oil
¼ tsp mustard seeds
A pinch of cumin powder

Method

1. Combine all the ingredients and grind to a paste.
2. For the seasoning, heat the oil and fry the mustard seeds till they stop spluttering. Then add the cumin powder.
3. Remove from heat and pour it over the paste.
4. Serve.

Kai (Hand-patted Roti)

Ingredients

1 glass each of rice flour and gram flour
1 glass each of ragi flour and maize flour
3 glasses water
½ tsp turmeric powder
2 onions, chopped
5 green chillies
1 sprig coriander leaves, chopped
1 sprig curry leaves
½ tsp cumin powder
1 cup chopped greens (Kerai)*
Salt to taste

* Indian greens and sabbassagai available all over South India.

Method

1. Pour 3 glasses of water into a saucepan and bring it to the boil. Mix all the above ingredients slowly to form a thick dough. Stir and slightly cool. Make balls out of the dough. Grease the palm of your hand with a little oil and then flatten the balls into discs (rotis).

2. Heat the griddle and smear with some oil. Place the roti on it and cook. Turn over when cooked and golden on one side.

3. Serve with Vana Menchinkai chutney (recipe on page 17).

Vana Menchinkai Chutney

Ingredients

12 red dry chillies, soaked in water
6 cloves garlic
1/8 tsp cumin seed
1 sprig curry leaves
A marble-sized ball of tamarind
Salt to taste

Method

1. Place all the ingredients in a grinder and grind to a smooth paste.

Bisebelli Bhat

Ingredients

½ cup carrots
2 each of onions and capsicums
½ cup double beans
½ cup peas
½ cup oil
2 tbsp clarified butter
¼ tsp mustard seeds
1 lemon-sized ball of tamarind
1 tbsp jaggery, powdered
¼ cup coconut, grated
2 glasses water

Mysore Pak

Recipe on page no. 100

For the powder

1 cup Bengal gram lentil, 1 cup coriander seeds
20 red chillies
2 long cinnamon sticks
15 cloves

For the rice

2 cups thoor dhall
1 cup rice
Salt to taste

Method

1. Roast the ingredients for the powder lightly and grind into a semi-coarse powder.
2. Coarsely chop all the vegetables and keep aside.
3. Pour the oil in a vessel, fry the mustard seeds and then sauté the onions. Add the lentils, vegetables, rice and bisebelli bhat powder.
4. Pour 2 glasses of water and pressure cook for 7 minutes till it is well mashed.
5. Squeeze the juice out of the tamarind.
6. When the rice is done, remove the lid and mix the tamarind juice, jaggery and coconut in it. Mix well. To the hot bisebelli bhat add the clarified butter. Serve.

   (Bisebelli bhat is a speciality of Karnataka. No ceremony is complete without the Bisebelli bhat. This is equivalent to the Tamil Nadu Sambar Sadam.)

Huruli Saru

Ingredients

2 cups horse gram
¼ cup oil

For the Saru

¼ tsp cumin
½ copra, grated
1 onion, chopped
1 tomato
1½ tsp red chilly powder
2 tsp coriander powder
⅛ tsp turmeric powder
⅛ tsp mustard seeds and a few curry leaves for seasoning
1 bunch coriander leaves, chopped
Salt to taste

Method

1. Soak the horse gram overnight. Then strain and tie in a muslin cloth. Leave to sprout for 3 days.
2. Grind all the ingredients for the saru, except the seasoning.
3. Pour the oil in a wok and place over heat. Then add the seasoning and the ground masala paste. Gently fry the ingredients, add the sprouted horse gram, 2 cups of water and cook till tender. Add salt to taste.
4. Serve with plain boiled rice.

Madikai Kalu

Ingredients

1 cup dry kidney beans
1 onion, chopped
1 tomato, chopped
4 green chillies, chopped
¼ cup grated coconut
1 small bunch coriander leaves, chopped
⅛ tsp turmeric powder
Salt to taste

For the seasoning

3 tbsp oil
1 sprig curry leaves
¼ tsp mustard seeds
¼ tsp cumin

Method

1. Soak the beans overnight in water. Strain. For preparing the bean sprouts, tie them in a muslin cloth. Remove the cloth after 3 days. For preparing immediately, first wash the beans, then dry and finally roast them.

2. Pour the oil in a wok. When hot, add the mustard seeds, curry leaves and cumin. Also add the onion and the rest of the ingredients except the coconut and coriander and fry them.

3. Add the beans, pour 1 glass of water and cook over low heat till it reaches a thick medium consistency. Remove from the heat and add the grated coconut and coriander leaves. Mix well.

Note: To cook the roasted beans, pressure cook the beans for 10 minutes with sufficient water.

Thelli Saru

Ingredients

1 cup thoor dhall
6 tomatoes, chopped
1 cup water
½ tsp turmeric powder
A marble-sized ball of tamarind
1 tbsp jaggery

For the powder

1 tsp cumin
¼ cup black pepper
1 cup coriander powder
1 cup red dry chillies
½ tsp asafoetida

For the seasoning

2 tsp oil
⅛ tsp mustard seeds
1 clove garlic, coarsely crushed
A few curry leaves, coriander leaves for garnishing

Method

1. Roast the thoor dhall to a light golden.
2. For the thelli saru powder, roast the other masalas. When cool, grind to powder and bottle it for future use.
3. Pressure cook the thoor dhall, tomatoes and turmeric powder, along with water till done. Mash it well, strain and keep aside.
4. Squeeze out the juice from the tamarind. Then add the jaggery.
5. Add it into the dhall along with 1½ teaspoons thelli saru powder. Mix well.
6. Heat the oil in a vessel and add the ingredients for the seasoning. Then add the dhall mixture and bring it to the boil.
7. Remove from heat and garnish with the coriander leaves.
8. Serve hot.

Hallu Obutu

Recipe on page no. 101

Bayraikai Soppu

Ingredients

½ cup mixed greens of all varieties, chopped and cleaned
1 tbsp each of moong and thoor dhall
1 tbsp each of lobia and avarai belai
1 large onion, chopped
8 green chillies
2 tomatoes, chopped
1 clove garlic

For the masala

1 tsp coriander seeds
¾ tsp cumin
2 tbsp grated coconut
1 tbsp oil

For the seasoning
1 tbsp oil
A few mustard seeds

Method

1. Soak the dhalls overnight. Pressure cook the dhalls along with the other ingredients for 7 minutes.

2. Fry the coriander seeds, cumin and coconut in the oil and grind to a paste when cool.

3. Put the dhall mixture in a liquidiser and liquidise for a second, then add the ground masala paste.

4. For the seasoning, pour the oil in a vessel and add the mustard seeds. When they begin to splutter, pour into the dhall.

Batani Usili

Ingredients

1 cup dry peas
1 onion, chopped
8 garlic pods, chopped
6 green chillies, chopped
1 tbsp butter
½ coconut, grated
Coriander leaves, chopped
Salt to taste

For the usili powder

1 tsp fenugreek seeds
3 tsp cumin

Method

1. For the usili powder, roast the fenugreek seeds and cumin. Then grind to a powder and store in a bottle.

2. Soak the peas. Then boil them in water till they are tender.

3. Place a wok over heat, add the butter, then immediately add the chopped ingredients and fry gently. Add the usili powder, along with salt, coconut and coriander leaves.

4. Remove from heat and serve.

Mixed Vegetable Sagu

2 each of potatoes and carrots, chopped
½ cauliflower, chopped
1 cup tomatoes, chopped
⅓ cup oil
⅛ tsp mustard seeds
½ tsp besan dhall
1 onion, chopped
5 green chillies, chopped
2 tbsp coconut, grated
1 tsp kas kas, ground and roasted
A few curry leaves
Salt to taste

Method

1. Pour the oil in a wok. When hot, add the mustard seeds, besan dhall, onion, green chillies and curry leaves. Gently fry, then add the chopped vegetables and cook over low heat.

2. When half done, add the coconut and kas kas. Then add salt to taste and sprinkle curry leaves. Remove when the vegetables turn crisp.

3. Serve hot.

Ragi Mudde

Ingredients

1 cup water
¾ cup ragi flour

Method

1. Pour the water into a vessel and place it over heat. When the water comes to the boil add in the ragi flour. With a wooden spoon keep stirring to avoid forming lumps. Allow to cook. When the mixture starts steaming, remove from the heat.

2. Put the mixture of the ragi in a plate, then dip your hands in cold water and shape into round balls, the size of a tennis ball.

3. Serve with Bus Saru or Soppu Saru.

Mysore Mandya Upensa Saru

Ingredients

1½ cups water
½ cup thoor dhall
2 bunches of fresh greens or 1 cup chopped beans or any gourd
Salt to taste

For the chutney

4 green chillies
4 cloves garlic
1 small bunch coriander leaves
½ cup coconut, scraped

Method

1. Pressure cook the dhall and beans or greens separately. Strain both and keep aside.

2. Grind all the ingredients for the chutney to a smooth paste and keep aside.

3. Serve the dhall, beans or greens and chutney with ragi mudde or plain rice.

Kesari Bhat

Recipe on page no. 103

Bus Saru

Ingredients

¼ cup oil, ⅛ tsp mustard seeds
¼ cup each of black gram lentil and Bengal gram lentil
3 red chillies, broken
2 cloves garlic, pounded and crushed with skin
1 big onion, chopped
2 sprigs curry leaves

For the masala
½ tsp cumin seeds
¼ tsp fenugreek seeds
1 bunch coriander leaves
2 sprigs curry leaves

1 clove garlic
1 big onion, chopped
¼ cup coconut, grated
2 tsp sambar powder
1 marble-sized ball of tamarind
Salt to taste

For the seasoning

1 tbsp oil
⅛ tsp mustard seeds
1 onion, chopped
A few curry leaves

Method

1. Pour the oil in a pressure cooker and add the mustard seeds along with the other ingredients. Pressure cook till the lentils are tender.
2. Grind all the ingredients for the masala.
3. Mix the lentils with the above ground masala.
4. Heat the oil and add the seasoning ingredients, then season the lentils.
5. Boil the lentils for a minute and remove from heat.
6. Serve with rice or Ragi Mudde (recipe on page 36).

Soppu Saru

Ingredients

1 cup thoor dhall
4 bunches of any greens
5 green chillies
1 each of onion and tomato
1 big clove garlic

For the seasoning

$1/_8$ tsp mustard seeds
1 tbsp oil
1 sprig curry leaves
Salt to taste

Method

1. Pressure cook all the ingredients in 1½ cups water for 6 minutes.
2. When done, liquidise the whole mixture slightly.
3. In a pan, pour in the oil, then add the seasoning ingredients, except salt, and cook for a few minutes.
4. Pour over the liquidised mixture and season with salt.
5. Serve with plain rice or Ragi Mudde (recipe on page 36).

Ragi or Akki Roti

Ingredients

1 cup tender drumstick leaves, chopped
1 cup coriander leaves, chopped
6 green chillies, finely chopped
2 onions, finely chopped
1 cup coconut, grated
1 tbsp groundnuts, roasted and powdered
2 cups ragi or rice flour
Salt to taste

Method

1. Add the flour to the above ingredients and mix well.
2. Add sufficient water to knead into a dough. Keep aside.
3. Shape the dough into lemon-sized balls. Roll into round discs like rotis. Soak your hands in cold water to pat the rotis.
4. Heat a griddle and fry the rotis, smearing a little clarified butter on both sides, till they turn light brown and crisp.
5. Serve with coconut chutney.

Hunsae Mentai Gojju

Ingredients

½ cup tamarind juice
1 cup small onion, chopped
1½ tsp red chilli powder
¼ tsp turmeric powder
1 tsp coriander powder
¼ tsp mustard seeds
½ tsp fenugreek powder, roasted
A little asafoetida
1 tbsp oil
Salt to taste

Method

1. Pour the oil in a wok, add the onion, mustard seeds and all the above ingredients except the tamarind. When fried, add the thick tamarind juice. Cook till it thickens.

2. Remove from heat and serve with hot rice.

Hasiru Chops

Recipe on page no. 52

Aloogadai Paliya

Ingredients

4 big potatoes
1 large onion, chopped
1 small bunch coriander leaves, chopped
1 clove garlic, chopped
1 tsp ginger paste
½ tsp garam masala
1 tsp each of coriander and chilli powder
2 tbsp oil
A little turmeric powder
⅛ tsp mustard seeds
⅛ tsp each of Bengal gram and black gram lentil
A few curry leaves
Salt to taste

Method

1. Clean the potatoes, peel and cut into rounds.
2. Cook over heat with salt and turmeric powder.
3. Place a wok over heat, pour in the oil, add the mustard seeds, black gram lentil and Bengal gram, curry leaves and onion. Add all the remaining ingredients and fry well.
4. Then add the cooked potatoes and fry gently without breaking them till the gravy is dry.
5. Serve hot.

Hasiru Chops

Ingredients

1 kg mutton chops
½ cup oil, 1½ cups water
2 onions, sliced
2 tomatoes, chopped
Salt to taste

For the paste

1 tomato, chopped
1 bunch each of mint and coriander leaves
1" piece each of ginger, cinnamon and garlic
8 green chillies
1 tsp pepper
4 cloves, 2 cardamoms

Method

1. Grind all the ingredients for making the paste and keep aside.
2. Heat a wok and add the oil.
3. Fry the onions and add the mutton chops. Then add the ground paste and salt to taste.
4. Add the tomatoes and water.
5. Fry well. Then transfer to a pressure cooker and cook for 15 minutes.
6. Remove the lid of the pressure cooker and simmer till the gravy has thickened. Serve.

Picture on page no. 49

Hurida Koli

Ingredients

1 kg chicken, cut into pieces
2 onions, chopped
1 clove garlic, chopped
1" piece ginger, chopped
2" piece cinnamon
¼ cup oil
4 cloves
1 tsp black pepper
1 tomato, chopped
2 tsp coriander powder
2 tsp chilli powder
Salt and turmeric powder to taste

For garnishing

Finely chopped coriander leaves and fenugreek leaves

Method

1. Place a wok over heat, pour in the oil and add the onions, ginger and garlic. Cook till the mixture turns brown in colour.

2. Add the rest of the ingredients along with very little water.

3. Pressure cook for 7 minutes. Fry the chicken well, add the coriander and fenugreek leaves and continue frying till it turns dry and brown.

4. Remove from pressure cooker and serve.

Hurada Handi Badu

Ingredients

1kg pork, cut into medium-sized pieces
2 tsp pepper powder
1 full garlic pod
1" piece ginger
1 onion, chopped
1½ tbsp coriander seeds, roasted
2 cups water
⅛ tsp turmeric powder
¼ cup oil
Salt to taste

Method

1. Grind all the ingredients to a smooth paste, except for the pork.
2. Pour the oil in a pressure cooker and fry the pork with the ground paste. After a while pour some water.
3. Cover and pressure cook the pork till it is dry. Stir-fry till it turns brown in colour.
4. Remove from the pressure cooker and serve hot.

Koli Saru

Ingredients

1 kg chicken, cut into medium pieces
1½ tsp red chilli powder, a little turmeric powder
1½ tsp coriander powder
4 cloves
1 large piece of cinnamon
2 onions, chopped
1 tomato, chopped
½ cup grated coconut, ground
1 bunch coriander leaves, chopped
¼ cup oil
1½ cups water
Salt and pepper to taste

Koli Saru

For the paste

2 onions, chopped
1" piece ginger
1 clove garlic
1 tsp black pepper
3 each of cardamoms and green chillies

Method

1. Fry the ingredients for the paste in very little oil. When cool, grind to a paste.

2. Add red chilli powder, turmeric powder and coriander powder to it.

3. Place a wok over heat. Pour the oil, sauté the onions and tomato and add all the spices. Add the ground paste and then add the chicken pieces.

4. Add salt to taste along with the water and cook the chicken for 7 minutes.

5. Remove the lid, and add the coconut, coriander leaves and pepper powder. Stir and remove from heat.

6. Serve hot.

Meenu Saru

Ingredients

1 kg well-cleaned fish, cut into slices or pieces
1 onion, chopped
1 clove garlic
1" piece ginger
½ cup coconut, grated
½ tsp fenugreek, roasted
½ tsp cumin
1½ cups water
2 tsp each of chilli powder and coriander powder
1 tomato, a little turmeric powder
1 marble-sized ball of tamarind
1½ tbsp oil

¹/₈ tsp mustard seeds
A few sprigs curry leaves
Salt to taste

Method

1. Grind together all the ingredients except the oil, mustard seeds, curry leaves, fish and onion.

2. Heat a wok, pour oil in it and fry the remaining ingredients except the fish.

3. Add the ground paste and fry again till the raw smell disappears.

4. Add the fish and some water. Sprinkle salt to taste and cook till done.

5. Serve.

Vanna Meenu Saru

Ingredients

½ or 1 cup avarai kalu
4 aubergines or potatoes, chopped
1 large dry fish piece
¼ cup oil
⅛ tsp mustard seeds
1 small onion, cut into slices
A few curry leaves
⅛ tsp turmeric powder
1 lemon-sized ball of tamarind
Salt to taste

For the paste

½ cup coconut, grated
1" piece ginger
1 onion
1 clove garlic

Method

1. Soak the avarai kalu overnight. Then cook it along with the aubergines or potatoes.

2. Clean the fish piece and remove the excess salt. Grind all the ingredients for making the paste.

3. Squeeze the pulp of the tamarind into the ground paste.

4. Place a vessel over heat, pour in the oil, add the mustard seeds, onions, curry leaves add the ground paste. Mix in the turmeric powder and salt to taste.

5. Add the cooked vegetables and fish and simmer till a medium thick gravy forms.

6. Serve with plain rice or Ragi Mudde (recipe on page 36).

Koli Bus Saru

Ingredients

1 kg chicken, cut into medium-sized pieces
1 cup green gram lentil or kadalai (soaked and partially cooked)

For the masala

1 tbsp coriander powder
2 tsp chilli powder
1 tsp black pepper
1/8 tsp turmeric powder
1 garlic, clove and 1 onion, chopped
1" piece ginger, chopped
1 cup coconut, grated
Salt to taste

For the powder

1 tbsp raw rice
1 tsp kas kas
5 red chillies

For the seasoning

¼ cup oil
1 onion, a few chopped curry leaves

Method

1. Grind the masala into a smooth paste.

2. Pressure cook the green gram (or the kadalai) and chicken along with the masala paste for 7-8 minutes. Remove from heat and strain. Keep the water aside, to be served with the main dish. Also keep the chicken and the green gram separately.

3. Add the ingredients for the powder and seasoning into the gram and chicken and toss well.

4. Pour the preserved water in a bowl and keep the chicken and gram in a dish.

5. Serve with Ragi Mudde (recipe on page 36).

Mamsa Pallav

Ingredients

1 kg mutton, cut into medium-sized pieces
1 kg samba rice, soaked for ½ an hour
1 cup oil, 3½ cups water
Juice of one lemon

For the paste

1 bunch each of coriander and mint leaves
1" piece each of ginger and cinnamon
4 each of cardamoms and cloves
2 onions, 2 cloves garlic
10 green chillies
1 cup coconut, grated
Salt to taste

Method

1. Grind all the ingredients for making the paste.
2. In a large saucepan, pour in the oil, add the mutton and ground masala. Fry well.
3. Then add 1½ cups water for the mutton to cook. When the mutton is tender, add the rice and the remaining water.
4. Sprinkle salt to taste. When the rice is cooked, add the lemon juice. Stir gently.
5. Serve hot.

Mamsa Pallav

Kanji

Ingredients

1 cup rice
3 cups water
2 tbsp clarified butter
Salt to taste

Method

1. Cook the rice with salt. Allow the thick rice water to remain. Add more water if necessary.

2. Pour in the clarified butter and serve with fish pickle, dry chicken or dry fish.

Neer Dosai

Ingredients

1 cup rice, soaked for 2 hours
1 tbsp coconut
½ cup oil
Salt to taste

Method

1. Grind the ingredients except the oil into a smooth batter.

2. Heat a non-stick dosai griddle. Smear it with half a teaspoon of oil. When the oil is hot, sprinkle a few drops of water on the griddle so that it sputters. Then pour two tablespoons of the batter on the griddle. Spread it outwards gently in a circular motion.

3. Cover and cook on low heat for a few minutes. Sprinkle oil along the edges if necessary. Make dosais in this manner with the remaining batter.

4. Serve with chutney (recipe on page 72).

Chutney for Neer Dosai

Ingredients

1 cup coconut, scraped
2 green chillies
2 cloves garlic
1 marble-sized ball of tamarind
1 tsp roasted black gram lentil
Salt to taste

For the seasoning

1 tsp oil
1/8 tsp mustard seeds
2 red chillies, broken
A few curry leaves

Method

1. Grind all the ingredients for the chutney to a smooth paste.
2. Heat the oil, add the ingredients for the seasoning and pour into the chutney and serve.

Basalae Aajdina

Ingredients

2 cups basalae leaves
A little salt
A little jaggery
1 tsp taal masala powder
1" piece ginger
1" piece garlic

For the seasoning

1 tbsp coconut oil
1 onion, chopped
Fenugreek seeds

Method

1. Cook the basalae leaves with salt, jaggery and taal powder. After a while add the ginger and garlic.
2. When cooked, mash the leaves roughly.
3. Pour the coconut oil in a wok, add the onion and fenugreek seeds. Season the basalae with it.

Note: This can be made with raw jackfruit, but add tamarind juice also along with the other ingredients.

Badanaikai Kodhel

Ingredients

½ kg aubergines, cut into 8 pieces and soaked in cold water
1 tbsp each of oil and grated coconut
8 red chillies
1 tbsp jaggery
½ tsp coriander seeds
¼ tsp each of cumin seeds and crushed garlic
2 cloves garlic
1 lemon-sized ball of tamarind
¼ tsp mustard seeds
A few curry leaves
1 tsp red chilli powder
Salt to taste

Method

1. Squeeze out the pulp of the tamarind in a glass of water.
2. Add salt and jaggery to it and keep aside.
3. Grind the coconut, red chillies, coriander and cumin seeds and garlic cloves to a smooth paste.
4. Take a vessel, pour in the tamarind liquid and place over heat. When it comes to the boil, add the aubergine pieces. After the aubergine pieces are cooked take them out.
5. Add the aubergine to the ground paste and cook for 5 minutes.
7. For the seasoning, heat the oil in a wok and add the mustard seeds, crushed garlic and curry leaves. Add the cooked aubergines and then the red chilli powder, mix as needed and serve.

Note: This can also be made with lady's finger, taking care not to add excess water.

Bajeel

Ingredients

1 cup beaten rice (Avalakki)
½ coconut, finely grated
2 tsp sugar
1 small onion, cut into pieces
1 tbsp hot clarified butter
1 tsp taal masala powder
Salt to taste

Fish Kari

Recipe on page no. 90

Method

1. Roast the beaten rice lightly.
2. Mix all the other ingredients well and add the roasted rice, along with the clarified butter.
3. Mix well again and serve.

Buns

Ingredients

½ kg flour
2 ripe bananas
½ cup curd
2 tbsp sugar
1 tsp cooking soda
2 tsp hot oil

Method

1. Place all the ingredients except the oil in a grinder and grind well.
2. Pour the oil into the flour mixture. Knead well into a soft dough. Cover and ferment this overnight.
3. Shape into rounds and roll out into thick discs and deep fry.
4. Serve with coconut chutney.

Koli Kari

Ingredients

1 kg chicken, cut into medium-sized pieces
½ coconut, grated and milk extracted
1 marble-sized ball of tamarind, juice extracted
1 tsp turmeric powder
1 tbsp coriander seeds
½ tsp each of cumin seeds and pepper
¼ tsp fenugreek seeds
20 red chillies
1 onion, chopped
2 tbsp coconut oil
Salt to taste

For the seasoning
2 tsp oil
1 chopped onion

Method

1. Roast the turmeric, coriander, cumin, pepper, fenugreek and red chillies in a pan, then grind into a smooth paste.

2. Spread the chicken on a plate and mix in the ground paste and salt.

3. Keep a pressure cooker over heat and pour in the coconut oil. When it begins to smoke, add the onion and chicken. Cook for a little while to get rid of the raw smell.

4. Pour 1½ glasses of water in it and pressure cook for 1 minute. When cooked, add the tamarind juice and coconut milk and simmer over low heat.

5. Season the onions in the oil and add to the curry. Serve hot.

Koli Aajdina

Ingredients

1 kg chicken, cut into medium-sized pieces
½ coconut, roughly ground
½ tsp cumin seeds
8 cloves garlic

For the seasoning
2 tsp oil
1 onion, chopped

Method

1. Follow the same steps as for Koli Kari (recipe on page 83).
2. When the chicken is cooked, add the coconut, cumin seeds and garlic.
3. Season as in the previous recipe.

Koli Taal

Ingredients

1 kg chicken, cut into medium-sized pieces lengthwise
8 cloves garlic
2 tbsp taal masala powder
2 tbsp thin coconut milk
1 marble-sized ball of tamarind juice extracted
½ coconut, thick milk extracted
or
½ coconut, coarsely ground

Method

1. Fry the chicken pieces till they turn light brown in colour. Add the garlic, taal masala powder and the thin coconut milk.

2. Fry for a while, pour in the tamarind juice and then the thick coconut milk. Cook till the chicken is tender and the gravy is thick.

Koli Taal

Fish Kari

Substitute 1kg fish, cut into medium-sized pieces in place of chicken. The ingredients and the method are the same as for koli taal (recipe on page 87), except for the seasoning. For this dish, one needs to season with sliced ginger, cumin seeds, fenugreek seeds and curry leaves.

Picture on page no. 79

Dry Fish

Ingredients

*1 cup dry prawns or fish, flaked or cleaned
A little oil*

Method

1. Soak the dry fish in water and remove excess salt.
2. Then dry and shallow fry the fish using very little oil.
3. Prepare the dry fish exactly the same way as the fish kari.

Fish Chutney

Ingredients

1 cup dry fish
8 cloves garlic
16 red chillies
½ coconut, grated
1 marble-sized ball of tamarind
Salt to taste

Method

1. Fry the dry fish. Roast the garlic, red chillies and coconut.

2. When cool, grind this without water along with the tamarind and salt. Then crumble the fish into small pieces, add to the ground mixture and mix well.

3. This chutney is best eaten with kanji made out of boiled rice or plain white rice.

Holigae

Ingredients

1 glass Bengal gram lentil
1 glass sugar
1 glass flour
2 cardamoms, crushed
½ glass oil

Method

1. Boil the Bengal gram in 2 cups water. Then grind it into a smooth paste with the sugar. Add the cardamoms.

2. Knead the flour with 2 tablespoons water and the oil into a soft dough. Keep the dough aside for 2 hours.

3. Shape the dough into balls and then flatten them. Fill each with one tablespoon of the gram mixture. Seal the edges and roll out into thin discs with a little oil smeared on the rolling board.

4. Heat a griddle and roast the discs on both sides till they become light brown in colour.

Jackfruit Payasa

Ingredients

2 coconuts, thick milk extracted
1 cup jaggery
1 cup jackfruit, diced
2 cardamoms, powdered

Method

1. In a saucepan, pour in the coconut milk and jaggery. Stir continuously over low heat.

2. When it comes to the boil, add the jackfruit pieces and cook slowly, till the pieces are tender. When done, add the cardamom powder.

3. Serve warm.

Jackfruit Gatti

Ingredients

4 glasses ripe jackfruit, ground
½ glass jaggery, crushed
1 glass rice
½ coconut, grated
A few large jackfruit leaves or teak leaves
Salt to taste

Method

1. Grind all the above ingredients together without water (except the leaves).
2. Place 2 tablespoons of this mixture on each leaf and steam.
3. Serve with Koli Taal (recipe on page 87).

Appi Payasa

Ingredients

1 litre milk, 2 cups sugar
2 cardamoms, powdered
Roasted almonds or cashew nuts and raisins

For the appis

1 cup flour
¼ cup fine semolina
½ cup water
Oil

Method

1. For the appis, knead the flour and semolina into a rough dough with water.
2. Shape into small balls and roll out into thin puris (small discs). Fry the discs in the hot oil.
3. Boil the milk and add the sugar. Lower the flame and stir till the milk thickens and is reduced to half. Remove from heat and add the crushed pieces of puris. Sprinkle cardamom powder, raisins and nuts over it.

Appi Payasa

Mysore Pak

Ingredients

1 tbsp gram flour
2 tbsp sugar
3 tbsp clarified butter

Method

1. Make a syrup of one-string consistency with the sugar and a little water.

2. Dry roast the gram flour in a wok. Add the clarified butter and sugar syrup very slowly, stirring the mixture all the time.

3. When the mixture leaves the sides of the wok immediately pour it onto a well-oiled plate. Do not flatten with a spoon or knife.

4. Shake the plate in a way that the mixture flattens and spreads by itself. After some time, when it is slightly cool, cut into pieces and serve.

Picture on page no. 19

Hallu Obutu

Ingredients

1 coconut, grated
2 cups sugar or jaggery
2 cups flour
Oil for frying
1 tbsp kas kas
5 cardamoms, powdered
1 tbsp rice
A few almonds, peeled

Method

1. Grind the coconut, kas kas and rice together. Keep aside.
2. Place a vessel over heat, and make a thick syrup with the sugar or jaggery and water. Add the ground ingredients and bring it to the boil. Keep aside to cool.
3. Knead the flour into a stiff dough. Roll out into puris (small discs) and deep fry in hot oil. Dip each puri into the sugar syrup mixture. Repeat with all the puris.
4. Garnish with almonds and serve.

Picture on page no. 29

Kesari Bhat

Ingredients

1 cup each of semolina and water
1½ cups sugar
1 cup clarified butter
1 tsp saffron dissolved in milk
½ cup almonds or raisins, chopped

Method

1. Pour the clarified butter in a wok. Fry the semolina till it turns light brown in colour. Add the water, stirring all the while. Then mix in the sugar.

2. When the semolina is well cooked, add the saffron milk. Cook till the mixture leaves the sides and the semolina looks like little beads.

3. Garnish with the almonds or raisins and serve.

Note: Bits of cooked puris can also be added.

Picture on page no. 39

Pudina Pallau

Ingredients

1 glass basmati rice
or
Samba rice
½ cup boiled chickpeas
Salt to taste

For the paste

1 cup mint
1" ginger piece
½ cup copra

For the seasoning
½ cup clarified butter
1 onion, chopped
½ tsp cumin seeds

Method

1. Partially cook the rice with a little salt. Strain and keep aside.
2. Grind the ingredients for the paste and keep aside.
3. Place a wok over heat. When hot, pour in the clarified butter and add the onion and cumin seeds.
4. Then add the chickpeas, the paste and salt. Mix with the rice. Keep warm in the oven for 5 minutes and serve.

Chitra Anna

Ingredients

1 glass rice
½ tsp mustard seeds
8 to 10 red chillies
½ cup coconut, grated
⅛ tsp asafoetida
¾ tsp jaggery
Salt to taste

For the seasoning

2 tbsp oil
¼ tsp mustard seeds
1 sprig curry leaves

1 tsp black gram lentil
4-5 red chillies, broken
1 tsp Bengal gram
1 tbsp groundnuts
¼ tsp turmeric powder
Salt to taste

Method

1. Cook the rice till done. Do not overcook.
2. Grind the other ingredients to a coarse paste and keep aside.
3. Place a wok over heat and pour in the oil. When hot, put all the ingredients for the seasoning. Then add the paste and fry. Mix well with the rice and serve.

Variation
Ingredients

1 glass cooked rice
1 raw mango, grated

Chitra Anna

½ cup fresh grated coconut
A little asafoetida
¼ tsp turmeric powder
½ tsp mustard seeds
1 tsp each of black gram lentil and Bengal gram
1 tbsp groundnuts
1 sprig curry leaves
A few chopped coriander leaves
Salt to taste

Method

1. Place a wok over heat and pour in the oil. When it begins to smoke, add the mustard seeds, black gram lentil, Bengal gram, groundnuts and curry leaves.

2. Then add the mango, salt, asafoetida, turmeric powder and coconut. Mix with the cooked rice and serve hot.

Vegetable Bhat

Ingredients

1 glass cooked rice
2 tbsp oil, ¼ cup beans
¼ tsp mustard seeds
1 tsp each of Bengal gram and black gram lentil
1 bunch chopped fenugreek leaves
2 big potatoes, cut into cubes
½ cup peas, 2 capsicums
½ cup cauliflower, chopped
Salt to taste

For the powder

½ cup coriander seeds
½ cup each of Bengal gram and black gram lentil
15-20 dry red chillies

1 cup copra
2" piece cinnamon
4 cloves
1/8 tsp asafoetida

Method

1. Grind all the ingredients for the powder coarsely.

2. Place a wok over heat. Pour in the oil and when it begins to heat, add the mustard seeds, Bengal gram and black gram lentil.

3. Add the fenugreek leaves and fry well. Then add the potatoes and cook till half done. Add the other vegetables and ½ cup water and cook till the vegetables are tender.

4. When done add 1½ tablespoons of the ground powder. Mix well for 2 to 3 minutes, then add the cooked rice.

5. Add salt to taste. If required add more powder and mix well.

6. Serve hot, garnished with cashew nuts.

Picture on page no. 119

Raw Gojju

Ingredients

1 pineapple or cucumber, cut into small pieces
1 tsp coriander seeds
8-10 dry red chillies
1 tsp Bengal gram
¼ tsp cumin seeds
1 tsp sesame seeds
½ cup grated coconut
1 marble-sized ball of tamarind
¼ cup jaggery, powdered
Salt to taste

For the seasoning

1 tbsp oil
¼ tsp mustard seeds
1 sprig curry leaves
A pinch of asafoetida
A little turmeric powder

Method

1. Pour a little oil in a griddle and fry the coriander seeds, chillies, Bengal gram, cumin and sesame seeds. Then grind to a fine paste with the coconut, tamarind and jaggery.

2. Place a wok over heat. Add the seasoning and the paste. Then add the pineapple or cucumber and salt to taste.

3. Mix well and serve.

Bayseeda Gujju

Ingredients

¼ kg lady's finger or ¼ kg aubergine or ¼ kg capsicum
¼ tsp fenugreek seeds
2 tsp black gram lentil
8 to 10 dry red chillies
1 tsp coriander seeds
½ tsp sesame seeds
1 marble-sized tamarind (pulp removed)
1 tbsp jaggery, powdered
¼ cup coconut, grated
Salt to taste

Method

1. Chop the vegetables into medium-sized pieces and fry them in the oil until tender.
2. Grind the remaining ingredients to a smooth paste.
3. Place a wok on heat, add the cooked vegetables and the paste.
4. Stir-fry for 5 minutes. Remove from heat.
5. Serve with rotis or hot rice.

Kuttu

Ingredients

Mixed vegetables (except lady's finger, aubergine or any other vegetable that squashes easily)
½ cup thoor dhall
½ tsp turmeric powder
¼ tsp black pepper
2" cinnamon stick
2 tbsp each of black gram and Bengal gram lentil
7 dry red chillies
2 tbsp coriander seeds
½ cup coconut, grated
1 marble-sized ball of tamarind
Salt to taste

For the seasoning

1 tsp oil
1/8 tsp mustard seeds
1/4 tsp asafoetida
A handful of groundnuts

Method

1. Cut the vegetables into small cubes and cook separately. Keep aside.
2. Pressure cook the thoor dhall with 1 cup of water and turmeric powder for 7 minutes.
3. Grind the rest of the ingredients.
4. Mix the cooked dhall, cooked vegetables and the ground ingredients after adding a little cold water to the ground ingredients to smoothen into a paste.
5. Bring the dhall to a boil on a low fire.
6. For the seasoning, heat oil in a wok and add the mustard seeds, a little asafoetida, a handful of groundnuts and fry. Add this to the dhall mixture.
7. This is now ready to eat with hot rice and clarified butter.

Vegetable Bhat

Recipe on page no. 111

Hayagriva

Ingredients

1 cup Bengal gram
¼ cup clarified butter
1 cup jaggery, powdered
2 cardamoms, powdered
¼ cup nuts, chopped and roasted
¼ cup copra, grated

Method

1. Pressure cook the Bengal gram in 1 cup water for 7 minutes.

2. In a wok, pour in the clarified butter and jaggery. When the jaggery melts, add the cooked dhall and nuts.

3. Then sprinkle the grated copra and the powdered cardamoms. Serve.